On the Scale, a Weighty Tale

For all the patient math teachers
I had growing up.
—B.P.C.

Weight:
The heaviness
of an object

A note about weight:
People in the United States and Canada have two systems to measure
weight. One is called the English system, or the U.S. customary system. It
uses ounces, pounds, and tons. The other system is called the metric
system, or International System of Units. It uses grams, kilograms, and
metric tons. People in many countries use only the metric system.

On the Scale, a Weighty Tale

by Brian P. Cleary

illustrated by Brian Gable

Ⅿ MILLBROOK PRESS / MINNEAPOLIS

A heavy backpack filled with books,

a teeny paper kite

a friend named Kate,
Who just turned eight—

these all **Weigh** something, right?

Weighing things is how we find the heaviness of stuff—

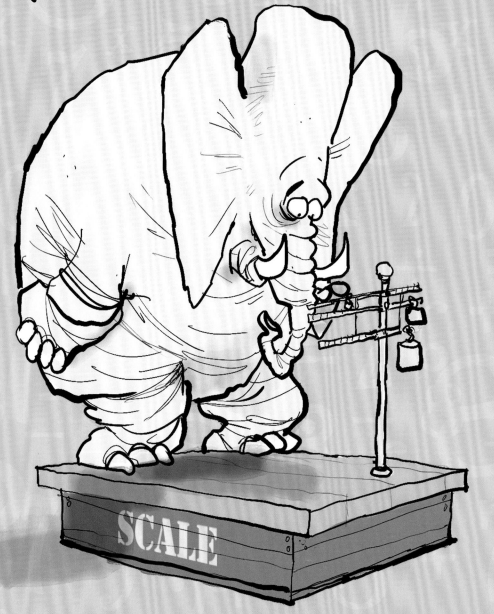

SCALE

a soccer ball,
great-grandma's shawl,

and bags of pillow fluff.

An ounce is just the thing to use for very light amounts.

That slice of bread
you've just been fed?

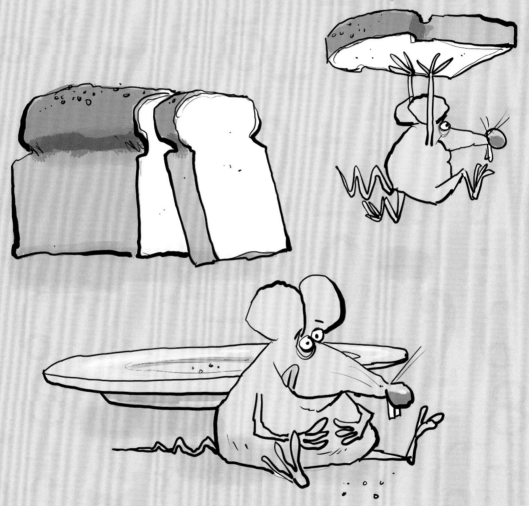

It weighs about 1 ounce.

16 ounces make 1 pound,

So picture sixteen slices.

They'd **weigh** around 1 single pound,

no matter what the price is.

The very heaviest of things
we talk about in tons.

Like trucks and trains
of ducks and cranes
or freighters filled with buns.

A ton is huge—

1 TON
2,000 POUNDS

it takes 2,000 pounds
to make just 1.

cars and whales upon the scales
are measured by the ton.

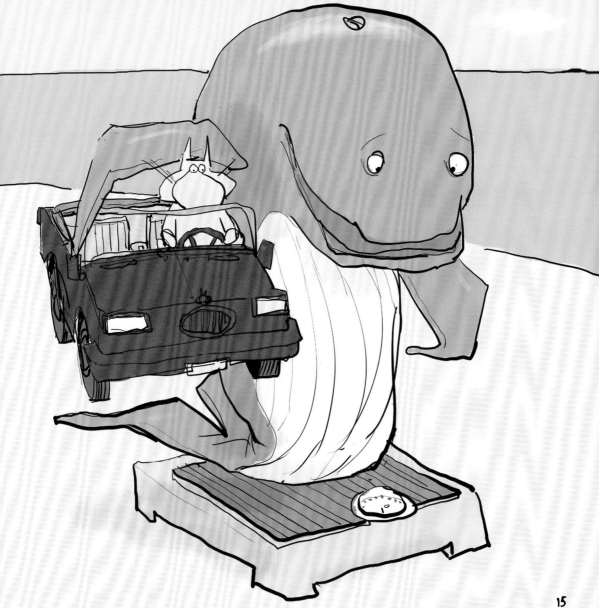

A scale is the tool we use to **weigh** things small and large.

Scales can measure a trunk filled with treasure,

a crate
or some bait

or a barge.

Having more than just one way to measure **Weight** is best.

Scales

So memorize each metric size,
and you'll pass any test!

A gram is not a cracker,

and it's not your parents' mothers.

It's a weight,
so get this straight—

it's smaller than most others.

A dollar bill or paper clip

Weigh near 1 gram, you know.

Inside 1 ounce, you can announce, there's 28 or so.

Take 1,000 of these **grams,**

and kilogram's the name.

A quart of milk, 2 pounds of silk,

each **weigh** about the same.

1,000 kilograms are what make up 1 metric ton—

about as heavy as a Chevy

(at least a smaller one).

to teach a class, because—alas—
you've learned a **TON** of stuff.

So, what is Weight? Do you know?

1 female giraffe weighs about 1 metric ton

4 large apples weigh about 1 kilogram

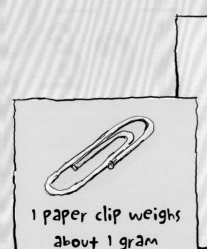

1 paper clip weighs
about 1 gram

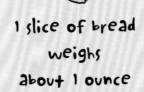

1 slice of bread
weighs
about 1 ounce

2 pears weigh
about 1 pound

English Weight Measurements
1 pound = 16 ounces
1 ton = 2,000 pounds = 32,000 ounces

Metric Weight Measurements
1 kilogram = 1,000 grams
1 metric ton = 1,000 kilograms, = 1,000,000 grams

1 female walrus weighs
about 1 ton

Find activities, games, and more at
www.brianpcleary.com

ABOUT THE AUTHOR & ILLUSTRATOR

BRIAN P. CLEARY is the author of the Words Are CATegorical©, Math Is CATegorical©, Food Is CATegorical™, Adventures in Memory™, and Sounds Like Reading™ series. He has also written The Laugh Stand: Adventures in Humor; Peanut Butter and Jellyfishes: A Very Silly Alphabet Book; The Punctuation Station; and two poetry books. Mr. Cleary lives in Cleveland, Ohio.

BRIAN GABLE is the illustrator of several Words Are CATegorical© books, as well as the Math Is CATegorical© series. Mr. Gable also works as a political cartoonist for the Globe and Mail newspaper in Toronto, Canada.

Text copyright © 2008 by Brian P. Cleary
Illustrations copyright © 2008 by Lerner Publishing Group, Inc.

Millbrook Press
A division of Lerner Publishing Group, Inc.
241 First Avenue North
Minneapolis, MN 55401 USA

For reading levels and more information, look up this title at www.lernerbooks.com.

Library of Congress Cataloging-in-Publication Data

Cleary, Brian P., 1959—
    On the scale, a weighty tale / by Brian P. Cleary ; illustrated by Brian Gable.
      p. cm. — (Math is categorical)
    ISBN 978-0-8225-7851-2 (lib. bdg. : alk. paper)
    ISBN 978-0-7613-4657-9 (eb pdf)
    1. Weights and measures—Juvenile literature. 2. Weight (Physics)—Measurement—Juvenile literature. I. Gable, Brian, 1949- ill. II. Title.
  QC90.6.C585 2008
  530.8'1—dc22   2007033670

Manufactured in the United States of America
5-42802-8690-8/15/2016